SUBJECT MATTER

Also by Baron Wormser

POETRY

The White Words (1983)

Good Trembling (1985)

Atoms, Soul Music and Other Poems (1989)

When (1997)

Mulroney & Others (2000)

PROSE

Teaching the Art of Poetry: The Moves (coauthor) (2000)

A Surge of Language: Teaching Poetry Day by Day
   (coauthor) (2004)

SUBJECT MATTER

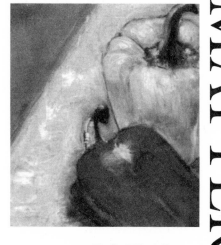

POEMS

Baron Wormser

Sarabande Books

LOUISVILLE, KENTUCKY

Managing Editor
Sarabande Books, Inc.
2234 Dundee Road, Suite 200
Louisville, KY 40205

Library of Congress Cataloging-in-Publication Data

Wormser, Baron.
        Subject matter : poems / by Baron Wormser.— 1st ed.
            p.   cm.
        ISBN 1-889330-97-3 (alk. paper) — ISBN 1-889330-98-1 (pbk. : alk. paper)
I. Title.
PS3573.O693S83 2004
811'.54—dc21   2003007376

Cover image: "Three Peppers" by Janet Wormser, 2001

Manufactured in the United States of America
This book is printed on acid-free paper.

Sarabande Books is a nonprofit literary organization.

FIRST EDITION

For Janet

and

For Howard Levy

CONTENTS

SUBJECT MATTER

ANECDOTES

A moment from a life—a husband holding up
A tee shirt for cursory inspection;
A child trudging home from a dull school day;
A tree in heavy wind—when placed within

The careful rails of verse acquires the dear,
Facile pout of meaning. It's a feeling
Rather than a faith since faith knows
Its way beforehand, while this telling is

A seeking. We read under the beneficence
Of a minor spell. Even the pain comforts:
Any life does; any avenue counts.
The man recalls a Sunday softball game;
The child stops at a puddle and peers into
Gorgeous nothingness; the tree falls or doesn't.

GLOBAL WARMING

Mumbling and joking, we hearken to pains
That fester in the comfort of unseasonable weather.
Our time is short—precisely. Uncertainties
Condole misgivings while we idle

In infinite traffic, drumming on plastic,
And imbibing sundry pert yet patient voices.
Good, good . . . and the sun was out yesterday.
How is it that the blanket that protects us

Feels more electric every year? Too many errands,
Too many longings—we could recount
Our flaws for hours but no one is asking.
We outlive insects but not trees.
Rocks are eternity. No snow tonight.
We unbutton a button, feel clammy, and comment.

BANKRUPTCY

The *condottieri* of money emblazon
Their glad-handing chicanery on frail paper,
Monumentalize their visions in acronyms.
When they go belly up, the good folk who

Dined on the crumbs, who rose each morning to
A mortgaged purpose, who applauded their own luck
Are saps, the everlasting fucked. Enough blame
To go around and blame gets around, though not

In high style. We want to while away a fortune
Pool side but how to get there legally?
Brains, brawn, seductive bodies: it's hot
In Texas and it gets to you. It fires you.
That unconditioned air is lethal. And when
It blows, every honky chateau implodes.

ISRAEL

Two dogs are sparring in a dusty street.
Two holy men dispute the nature of God.
A boy writes down that God is dog spelled
Backward, then looks with pleasure at his wit.

When his mother chastens him, he tells her that
He talks with God sometimes at night in bed
And God is okay with it. The boy plays in back
Of the house with a stick he calls a gun.

He waves it and aims it but doesn't fire.
The ghost of pity grazes his little brow.
The dogs are tireless but the onlookers
Drift away. Two old men in caftans remain.
Moody and silent, as if remembering,
They stare beyond each finite, impeded thing.

GENIUS

Extravagant, extra-vagant, so brilliant
The eye dazzles, falters, then hosannas
Its perturbed illuminations, so full of its
Indefinable self—ah, the Modernists

Knew how to set fire to an altar properly!
How to chew on their ashes? How to genuflect
With irony, how to indulge the mauves of piety?
Prolonged insouciance can be tiring.

We see Matisse kiss his pastel whims
And find further shores of sublimity.
That was Painting; the era was Before-The-
Next-Great-Thing. Breezily/uneasily we stand
Outside MoMA. One person goes by, another.
Sunlight turns the sidewalk into spatter.

ANTI-DEPRESSANT

What a pig happiness is. Plus
I'm a body living with an anti-body.
You probably don't know how that goes.
One of my hang-ups is my trying to tell you:

The pills tell me to let sincerity lapse.
I used to talk a true blue streak but now
I honor mute science as dryly as
The next atheist. I'm chemical

And it hurts. The calibrations come and go;
Research works overtime. I should be pleased
And some days am. It wavers and feints
And my smile is ghastly but I can walk down
A street and see the ratty English sparrows
Foraging in the litter and not start to cry.

BUDDHISM

It's about not-about. I'll start again
And stop there—which is more like it.
The Via Negativa goes Nowhere
And that's a beautiful place—the empty lake

In front of the barren hotel where some timeless,
Karmic habitués look past one another.
Better five minutes of Zen than
A hundred books about Zen. Poems

Are another story. They too inhabit
No place gracefully. They too dwell
Offhandedly in mini-eternities.
They too welcome oblivion. Authorship's
A drag but that too fades. Sit still again.
No nothing. You can feel it. Approximately.

FLYING

I tend to feel pretty pressured already
So when I sit there in my scrunched-up seat
That makes me feel like a mummy and I try
To open the small, sealed pouch containing

Maybe eleven wizened peanuts and can't,
I could flip. Except I'm busy holding my breath
Because my head's ready to split from
The sphere I've entered and my ears are thick

With crisp, brown noise. Faces smile warily.
I think of the earth and how I love to walk on it:
My legs describe a thesaurus of motion.
The wired are checking their messages
But I hear Fate's tocsin importuning—
Spry as a zealot, terse as malfunction.

10

DOT COM

Liked ginger beer and drank it from the bottle.
Stanford? Early software wave? Lost track
Of her languages. Do I talk only in phrases?
Hope not. A kind of cyber short hop sets in:

You get used to clipped synapse syntax.
You stare at pixels and they're talking.
You talk to people at meetings and they're
Tomb silent. Sounds like undergrad paradox.

I used to write a mean five-part essay.
Post-start-up but pre-merger? As a boy, I enjoyed
MONOPOLY and am familiar with play money.
Got it! She took the severance and split.
I'm changing life on earth and change is for
The better. Look at what people did before.

CHILDREN

"Okay" is the operative word, added
To the end of any parental decision and said
In a rising tone that is part question,
Part good-natured command, part mental

Temperature taking. The busy child looks up
Balefully. It isn't "okay" at all, this leaving
And coming, this eating and not eating, this lying down
And rising up. It presages the pangs of the existential,

The mortal and the Biblical—what is visible,
If unnamable, on beseeching adult faces.
No wonder the land of play beckons,
A haven from peremptory thought,
Where grown-up words and looks evaporate,
Where joy is nonsense you chant to yourself.

OBSCENITY

"Rage" is a word, hence more mental lint,
Hence one more reason to start swearing
Or never stop, which is what it sounds like
Many days in the bawling, crowded hallways.

Civility feels oversold until you lose it.
Meanwhile, the words are at once mace
And armor, warding hurt off, mocking it,
And mining the mother lode. Oh, brothers and sisters,

I curse you all: in the purple bruise
Of a dark, winter, tenement morning,
In the sunlight of the virulent noonday,
And the cool languor of evening. Together let
Us spar over nothing, greet each other brazenly,
And taunt the stammers of the peaceable.

WASHINGTON

Dead similes hope for a last fix—you see them
In the corridors clutching their tropes and looking
Around bravely: "This bill is like Swiss cheese;
It's full of holes. This bill is like fine wine gone bad.

This bill. . . ." Language reverbs, oscillates
Between manic and ludic. Do we think in words?
Or are they minions of appetite, brazening
And ordaining the venal complacencies?

Is there government without speechifying?
You can see the phrases—diligent sprites—line up
As another senator rises and starts to yawp.
Lowell evoked Rome but the high-mindedness
Of these propounders is American Puritan.
Any rhetoric had better be a bargain.

14

ELEGIES

Of an age, looking backward seems
The most natural view. The miserable tidiness
Of death does this, also the bone-cry
Of loss that won't be sweet-talked or soft-shoed,

That craves to convey the weight of what was.
Childish. A sort of petulance, a stamping of feet,
As if the heat of imagination could turn
"No" into "now." The words, of course,

Could not care less. They gather like hymn notes,
Birds in trees at dusk, beads of water.
Small sums come to seem precious
Because they are, and, as they are written
And spoken, they proclaim the brittle
Present and how it won't be contained.

TRUCKING

"He's pretty good-humored when he's not surly,"
That's Peckerwood talking about J.D., though
It could be Moonwalk talking about Bear Man,
Or Dropkick on Tail Feather. Thousands of miles

Space a mind out until there are gaps that feel
Like whole time zones where you forget who's there
Back home or that there is a back home.
When you're sitting somewhere getting weighed

Or a waitress forgets it was a double cheeseburger,
Your head springs back like a rubber band
And you feel how damn tired the body is
That supports your drifting mind. And when you call
Home and she's supposed to be there and she isn't,
Every crappy, twanging song becomes your own.

16

ANTHRAX

Fear doesn't make for second thought,
It makes for dread, that creaky,
Uneven, back step of consciousness.
Of an evening we've sat like children

Listening for monsters—the grave footsteps,
Hell treading the earth and pausing.
We've harangued evil with avid daylight,
Then pleaded in the dim confessional.

Invention improves. Techno-Shakespeare's
Iago must summon a further frailty.
Routine griefs and maladies pale.
The storms of villainy chitter and mope:
Words no longer compose speeches.
The phantasmal is real and vice-versa.

ROMANCE

Cutting through the fog banks of urbanity
Takes more than one but less than two martinis.
Within that zone the glimmer of a smile
Begins that might come to illumine a heart—

A metonymy for the random rivers
Of feeling coursing through human bodies.
Dim lights, extended hands above then
Below the table, a murmuring piano:

No wonder the moment is feted while
The lifetime is consigned to duration's
Gray dustbin. Outside, the traffic throbs,
Newsboys rumor, dusk settles into
Vacant evening. Simultaneously, both
People say something tender but witty.

KARMA

The psychological fissures craze
And deepen until a crevice can devour
An empire. A dowager is drinking tea
And looking out a window at the dregs

Of winter when her son rushes into
The room waving a pistol. "You did this to me,"
He exclaims. He aims the gun at her,
Then at himself, then at the window.

He begins to weep. She shakes her head and feels
The scales of age. She once was young and hailed
The phoenix of freedom. That was two wars ago,
A revolution, several marriages.
How many clever men has she known,
Who laughed and crowed and cracked like ill-fired clay?

KARMA (II)

Driving home from the second shift and thinking
About how Sandy Banks is always
Late on her paperwork, she sees a car
Heading toward her, going the wrong way

Up the ramp fast. She jerks onto the shoulder.
In a dark wind the car shoots by. No one's
Behind her and when she turns her neck around
To see, the car is gone already. She feels

A chill take hold of her; then she's shaking
And crying. The engine continues its chanting.
So strange, how her last thoughts
And final moments were like the rest
Of life, rooted in a deep narrowness.
She exhales, looks ahead—no lights before her.

INSPECTIONS

After we had washed and dried the dishes,
My sister or I marched into the living room
Where our stepmother sat scouring the paper
And asked her if she'd like to check our work.

A formality. She would come in regardless
And hold a glass up to the too bright
Kitchen light or consider a spoon or, better,
The spaces between the tines of a fork

For flecks of food. Cleanliness was next
To craziness, my sister and I used to say.
Praise and blame were strangely indifferent;
The rapt inspecting was everything.
We stood like middling soldiers, staring at
The worn floor she mopped each afternoon.

21

ORGASM

"If you don't know how to make me come,
Forget it. I'm not a receptacle,"
She offered by way of forthright
Declaration. 1979

In a singles bar somewhere on Long Island.
I wondered if she carried a manual.
She looked at my crotch as if
Appraising melons at the A & P.

"Actually," I countered, "I'm into foreplay.
I can make you melt before entering."
She looked at me quizzically, then rallied.
"Bullshit. I know that line, Mistuh Hot
Rocks. I'm outta here." I turned to the house band.
Frills and glitz. Every heartthrob was dying.

NATIONS

Like thuggish uncles they preen for their familiars,
Drape their oily sentiments with the flags
Of rhetoric, make a show of fairness:
They love the ugly parliaments equally.

Menace resides beneath the practiced surface:
They wouldn't let another bloke of a state
Scupper them. Their callused fists show how
They would back up what were—at first—mere words.

Like uncles they are beloved for their good
And bad points. They never marry.
To be who they are they must be solitary.
Some seem to live forever and guard their looks
Jealously. They wear corsets for the photographs,
Then sit unfettered with a beer, bragging.

BEATS

Denominated by manic, hurt sincerity
Coupled with lust coupled with going places
In cars and looking out the windows at
The passing landscape and exclaiming

And standing on roadsides underneath what used
To be called the heavens and pissing coupled
With strangely classical affinities
Born of long afternoons in public libraries

Finding out about Goethe and Dante and Shelley
Coupled with intimations of spirit
Abiding in flowers, dogs, men, and women,
All specks of matter shaking in the blaze
Of eternity coupled with staccato, up-all-night
Talking: Jump. Dig. Bop. Go.

MOVING PICTURES

You sit in darkness and suspend your body
In the tenebrous ether of imagination.
The camera chaperones your eyes; the music
Telegraphs feelings. You are in a wide tunnel.

Even as a child this trance troubled me,
How it holds you so raptly and won't
Let go, how it never looks around
For the sake of looking. If you surrender,

You will be transported. My shortcoming,
No doubt, a clot in my soul. I like to sit
In a bar or coffee shop or diner and watch
The people around me. The lights hum amid
Laughter, silence, and deep small-talking.
Woe drums its fingers. You leave when you please.

TATTOO

Small butterfly high up on her left buttock
So that when I took her from behind
I could see it move. Once, I asked her about it,
How she had one that she couldn't see.

"Honey, that's the point," she told me.
We parted ways but I think of her and it
Sometimes when I'm with a lot of clothed
Humanity, in an airport or stadium,

And I can feel all that various, sighing flesh
Sitting and walking and standing. I start wondering
What tales, faiths, and whims have been impressed
Upon their skins. Names, mottoes, and most enticing,
The fey and grisly images that picture a feeling,
That embody a body's inky hunger for sense.

BLURBS

"Stylish" means not hopelessly hokey.
"Radiant" means uplift.
"Brilliant" means hyper-articulate
But vastly uncommunicative.

"Brave" means still breathing.
"Bighearted" means fuzzy.
"Dynamic" means overbearing.
"Wise" means self-satisfied.

"Taking risks" means receives a check
Biweekly but makes obeisance to
Rimbaud in a veiled corner of the soul.
"Triumphant" means a hack who hung in there.
"Luminous" see "Radiant."
"Bravo!" means I'm done with words.

SOLDIER

He kept a copy of Fitzgerald's translation
Of the *Iliad* with him and read it at odd hours:
"Between dying," as he put it, though he knew
There was no between. When pals in the squadron

Asked him what he was reading and he
Replied "war," they rolled their eyes and swore.
"Listen to the story," he would say and beckon
The buried parries of Hector and Achilles.

The night quaked with flares, metal shrieks
And cackles dwarfing any human plea.
The book remained a thick, consoling weight:
"Glory" no longer was a word, hence these words.
The cities burnt, the ships vanished on the heartless sea,
The iron din of blood wept timelessly.

GREAT PLAINS

As children we lay on the ground and let the wind
Flow over us. On our backs we looked up at
The deep-seated sky and felt dust darken our eyes.
On our stomachs we gripped the earth and heard

The ground groan. When we returned to our homes
That huddled by some spindly trees, we felt
Abandoned: any structure seemed false.
The purple sunsets smothered us.

How to stand up? How to take the wind in your chest
And not huff and choke? When Henry Spotted Horse
Collapsed on Main Street one autumn afternoon,
I looked down cautiously. His eyes were staring
In different directions. "Son, you have to live for
Hundreds of years before you know anything."

FARMHOUSES, IOWA

Invariably, a family in each one
And someone opening a refrigerator to get
A carton of milk, someone sitting in
A chair and shelling peas, someone looking

Out a window at a barn, two willow trees.
To image the feeling that can manage
The solitude seems wholly epic.
Children and parents and a grandmother

Sit around the dinner table: the parents
Up-since-dawn tired, the grandma muttering
About the half-thawed rolls, the children
Speaking all at once, then silent. In the parlor
A whiskey tumbler sits beside a Bible.
The old collie whimpers when a car goes by.

FARMING

Last acts, last rites, the acid of conclusion:
Like a snuffling dog I nose my way back—
Ned pulling the trigger of his old deer rifle
Seems to banish each prior moment

But doesn't, since moments have their own lives,
Like the brindled cats in the milking shed
Or the flies on the cow shit or the disconnected
Dotting of black-eyed Susans in the June fields.

"What's sweeter than fresh-cut hay?" Ned would ask,
Smiling when he stepped down from the tractor after
Endless hours. "Green perfume," he called it.
"What's sweeter?" I ask myself without bitterness:
Days and nights in his small, snug barn,
The bovine heat, the slow steps, each act done right.

Los Angeles

"So easy to parody it's not worth the effort,"
According to a friend who in his current
Career incarnation labels himself
"A softcore day trader." Paradise gone wrong,

Also, though paradise went that route
A while back despite the big promo.
No movie yet about John Milton's imaginings,
But you never know—angels are hot these days.

Trolls, war, sex, small towns, sex,
Big city, spies, sex, old hippies, sex:
Reality is a cinematic canard—
Nothing exists until it's been filmed.
Images colonize our vast heads.
Eden never was a place to live.

POET

For starters, she had seven cats ("Among
Poetry's sources is the holy mythos
Of numbers") none of whom was particularly
Likeable ("Poetry isn't eager to please").

She offered a bag of tea, forgot the sugar
And milk but poured herself a shot
Of something ("Flasks are a dying amenity")
Into her cracked, dainty, less than clean cup.

When I began to ask a harmless question, she
Peremptorily shushed me ("Interrogations
Are for academics and policemen") and proceeded
To describe a walk she had taken the prior
Afternoon that featured a memory of
A former lover ("Who didn't look like you").

GUNS

Without them, harum-scarum lacks go get 'em.
Arguments—frustration and cross purpose
Being the milk of human blindness—lack fright.
It's only words and most of that is swearing.

Though a gat helps Hamlet-types make
Snap decisions, no one is very Shakespearean.
It's more like Living Theater—waving a metal
Flag makes a queasy body feel better.

They're usually used on family, friends,
And one's gaping self. Still, if whatever
Bogeyman (or woman) shows up, there's solace
In feeling ready. The tabloids could come true.
Meanwhile there's the delicious, earnest heft,
The charm of murderous potency.

JOURNEY TO THE EAST

The guru was too fond of antitheses—
The further this / the less that—
For my hardened taste, but when we sat
Stilly I felt an unconcern for the clamor

Inside me that answers whatever
Cognition the world proposes.
An ant walked along his arm and he
Asked of it, "Who are you?" Stock wisdom

But he didn't move to brush the creature away.
Say, you or I are that ant crawling
Across a soft, somewhat hairy surface
And our instincts lie in our being alive
And that is all we know. What name is there?
What if great love is anonymous?

MYSTERIES

The clues scatter, disperse, but remain
Clues as a word or look or kiss
Seeds itself in the loam of inquiring memory.
In mysteries the gumshoe's attention turns

Not only to murder's gruesome formalities—
But to the byways of attentive satori,
How an unwilling phrase, grimace, lisp
Or stutter moves the fast-talking mind

Into a labyrinth that as it grows steeper
Grows clearer. The walls distend but
The skein of motive billows and illumines
The bleakest, shit-infested alley where
Another shabby heart mutters regrets,
Where the self's roar is the basic death.

36

OLD MOVIES

Wasting a few more hours of my mortal stint,
I watch for the half-dozenth time a comedy
From the 1930s in which people walk
Into swinging doors, flirt, and trade wisecracks

That even then were considered corny.
The men wear hats; the women wear dresses.
I, who have never believed for a half-second
In progress, could not care less: style never dies.

When I tell my office mate how I spent
My evening, she asks what's up with me
That I enjoy such retro trash. "There's work
To do," she says, and I know she means it in
More ways than I can count. I look at her
And feel my folly. I wish we had a camera.

CHANNEL 37

"Watch that crap and you'll start to believe it,"
My wife says as I sit dull-eyed yet tense.
I press *Off* to resume my practice of Rilke.
How long ago was that, the Age of Frantic

Purity, the Onslaught before the Debacle?
When did the noise of News supplant the wink
Of gossip? I've got crises up the yin-yang.
I fidget with electro-info angst—

Random metaphor with a tragic dent.
Perhaps the poet would find something to hymn,
Perhaps he wouldn't. He chases the negatives
And vanishments, such are their spectral charms.
I've got a mind of bombs. I wouldn't know
A lyre if I fell over it. No myth.

INDIAN

The sky has been screaming for centuries.
The creeks blanch and writhe with unknowing.
All creatures received the bones of death
And were tutored in the paths of thankfulness.

Standing in a graveyard in South Dakota,
I gaze at the winter earth and simple markers,
Then in each direction into fitful space.
My mind mutters to itself but nothing matches:

Unfettered spirit can't be taught. When I
Climb back in the rented van, that sad engine—
Purpose—resumes. There's no ghost dance
On the radio; a small town voice brays
With self-contentment. I need to sit in a bar
And plead with any god that I can find.

CHRISTMAS

Celebration becomes stupefaction
And when we sit in church our minds wander
To the little tree and our transferred bounty.
"Miracle" feels like the farthest of words:

You couldn't drive there in the fastest car.
It's numberless. Standing in a line
Or coming out of a store, a tincture of joy
Arises from what seems like nowhere:

Something that happened so long ago,
Something that has always been a good rumor,
Something that didn't use the front door
Is central and in its raw beauty unbearable.
I forget my business. When I look up at
The winter stars, I could begin to repent.

40

IRONY

Sideways longueurs and stutters stud
The otherwise hairy, straight ahead chest
Of much-exercised Existence. Bummer.
Just when you get the drift of some regime

It goes under, leaving you on another shore
Sniffing yet another cosmos of rules and regs.
Little wonder certain émigrés walk
Around with their eyes cast down and their smiles

Turned inward. How well they knew certain
Species of idiocy—speeches, choruses,
Congresses, a whole paraphernalia
Of routine disgrace and acerbic patience. Gone.
The grinning neon winks its bright subtext.
They dawdle and ponder. A vast sky sighs.

ROAD

Oblivion is a big, long welcome.
When Hank or Louise doesn't return
From the convenience store, motive lies
Not only in the personal griefs and angers

That hone their own brooding fuel
But in the lorn miles that beckon like love.
It's temporary—but what isn't?—
And it may be that what was sought

Was not so much escape as wonder:
The chance to feel a bit of immensity
And let it remind the soul how reduced
It had become. The rivers and peaks,
The forests and valleys correspond:
Inwardness is not always alone.

CLOUDS

Self-satisfaction doesn't do it, which
Is okay on both sides, poetry never wanting
The sheen of public opinion, most people glad
To glide, shuffle, loll, or run without

Its oblique assent. In schools it's medicine
Whose meaningful shiver is good for you—
Drink it down like a stoic, weasel a glimmer
Of sense, spew it like deft confetti.

It wanes and wizens and cumbersome prose resumes.
Children gaze out grimy windows at clouds
Coursing like wisps of moments across the sky.
No people live up there but words can be tossed there—
Bouquets of prescient air. Silly, of course,
But that never stopped love or beauty.

COMMUNIST

One night while frying *latkes* my mother told me
She had considered becoming a communist
In the Thirties. "Roosevelt was a politician
And America was Henry Ford and that anti-Semite,

The radio priest. I didn't though." She laughed.
"Probably, I didn't like any of the guys
Well enough." She laughed again. "I didn't
Believe in explanations either." I snickered

In the fullness of my intellectual sixteen-
Year-old self. I'd read *The Eighteenth Brumaire*
And looked around on the bus in the morning for
Wage slaves though I was looking in other ways too.
Pimples Hurwitz stared at my books and said that
History was about getting laid. Sagely, I concurred.

TRAGEDY

Imagine the land, rock, sky putting a hand
On you that doesn't let go, that holds you
In awful vastness. The human occasion
Lacks confirmation. The emptiness calls

No one's intimate name and any answer
Is dumb as a cactus and cold as nightfall.
When a hero appears the gathered
Soldiers are more sullen than vengeful.

The dignity of the dispossessed dogs them;
The jokes they trade about braves and squaws
Never placate them. Even death fails.
When Crazy Horse stands before the flag-topped fort,
They wonder what led them to this time-scoured spot
And whether his fierce eye will ever leave them.

BLUES

Blues came round and knocked on my back door
Oh blues came round and knocked on my back door
Hello, Mister Blues, I've seen you before

Some folks' kindness always comes with a speech
Oh some folks' kindness always comes with a speech
Every long day, they got something to preach

My woman left me, that's a natural fact
Oh my woman left me, that's a natural fact
She told me her good heart is not coming back

Talking and drinking only make it worse
Oh talking and drinking only make it worse
You enter naked and you leave in a hearse

Morning and evening are a dance on stark ground

Oh morning and evening are a dance on stark ground

A power you borrow before you go down

Restaurant

"The only art to prosper in the postmodern age,"
According to more than one weighty wag,
The stomach remaining one locale
Where imagination must placate need.

The adjectives of possibility glow softly
As diners fondle and relish expectation,
Then, in the munching act, forget, for a time,
The rawer plagues of consciousness.

In the delicious lethargy of after-the-meal
The mind is free to admire, among burps
And sighs, the wages of satiation.
Occasionally, someone quotes Eliot
About a very good dinner. The others ponder
Their empty plates. Transcendence can wait.

DISASTERS OF WAR

Three empty-eyed heads balance delicately—
Wooden flowers, they snap in a sudden gust.
Look! They have emptied their notions onto
The ground in front of them. That small puddle.

Their high-pitched voices tremble and waver.
Their mouths explode and their faces break into
Shivers of lead. This moment is forever.
Whatever is said about loss is a lie of words.

Birds hear the wails and refuse to roost,
Small animals smell the human presence.
Now the bodies seize one another
And shake like a building a missile hits,
Like a shaman in ecstasy, like rutting stags.
Everything is spinning; then they fall down.

ATLANTIC CITY

Everyone is money and once you see
The ever ferreting human hand in that
Green, go-ahead light, then the trinkets,
Dice, and faux opulence have an almost

Metaphysical corollary: everything
Is moving—a thought normally
We push away but one here we rake in
Gladly. Happiness is social and iffy:

It wants to announce itself and it wants
To press against the electrostatic of other
Yearning psyches. We crowd around the tables
To absolve the maxims of betterment.
The self is much too predictable company;
We want luck's thrill to come and claim us.

50

GOD

Everything can't speak for Itself.

Neither can Nothing.

Infinity needs a medium.

Back when God was speaking He said

To keep it simple, stupid.

We didn't listen—our prerogative.

Instead, we interpreted.

We filled in the Blankness.

Once God committed himself to the Word

He must have known it was all over,

That this was a hall of mirrors

To perpetually mock

The long, sad face of Eternity.

Maybe, He smiled. Out of Mercy.

COMMUNE

"Energy Parcel Passing Through" was how
Arnie Elfman, also known as Cosmo,
Designated himself—as in "I'm just
An Energy Parcel Passing Through but I think. . . ."

We bore with it, as all of us were indulging
Some species of spiritual Quixotism
But one evening after a typical day
Of fixing broken machines, random squabbling,

Whole grains, and weather watching, Kate Scharf
Told Arnie/Cosmo/Energy she was tired
Of his self-conscious unconsciousness: "Who
In the name of Vishnu do you think you are?"
Arnie smiled cryptically and left the next morning.
He'd never been much help milking the goats.

VANITY

Vomiting almost casually into a men's room
Toilet, Richard confessed between spasms
That one too many Manhattans always
Did this. "By now I should be smarter."

Fifty-six was his "by now," but sums
Had never been his suit. He liked moments
And, at most, episodes. "If you started
Counting every casual trick, you'd be

Permanently sick." He wobbled to a mirror
Above a sink and considered his shaky self.
"Pallor looks good on me, I think," he said
And coyly winced. On the trip upstairs he held
Onto the rail tightly but when he reached the door
He strode into the loud, indifferent room.

OPINION

Halfway to work and Merriman already has told me
What he thinks about the balanced budget, the Mets'
Lack of starting pitching, the dangers of displaced
Soviet nuclear engineers, soy products, and diesel cars.

I look out the window and hope I'll see a swan.
I hear they're bad-tempered but I love their necks
And how they glide along so sovereignly.
I never take the time to drive to a pond

And spend an hour watching swans. What
Would happen if I heeded the admonitions of beauty?
When I look over at Merriman, he's telling Driscoll
That the President doesn't know what he's doing
With China. "China," I say out loud but softly.
I go back to the window. It's started snowing.

AUTHORS

His parents—father, a minister; mother,
A schoolteacher, both nodding flowers in
The breeze of accepted wisdom—liked to cite
William Makepeace Thackeray by way

Of acknowledging the cultural furniture
They favored—the capacious British novel.
The years did what? Faded? Frayed? Ripped
Along some teleologic fault line?

He found himself staring at a newspaper
And loathing the sexed squalor of Elvis Presley.
So much fine building to make such paltry dust.
Even the mildly epic Galsworthy down
The drain. He had listened but heard no gurgle
Of outraged time. How he yearned to remain.

DICTATOR

The signatures of random selfhood go nowhere:
They doze behind a bureau a grandma bestowed
An aeon ago; they gather dust on the plains
Of once familiar pages; they vomit

The lethargy of hope. Instead, the kind
Leer of a steel paterfamilias hovers
Like a zeppelin. Again and again,
News clips declaim the same fond poisons.

A no-longer-young woman looks up
At the banners, hears the amplified anthems,
And wonders what happened to her light steps
As she strolled beside the spangled river
On a spring evening, full of a little poetry,
Untutored by stature, happy by un-design.

BLOOD

The poet speaks of "the eloquence of blood" beside
Which "words are empty." "The martyrs," he says
"Are brave and almost holy." It's an old story
Though one I can understand: beside death

Language is inexcusable rhetoric.
Still, I marvel how the poet's phrases
Leap from his always-articulate tongue.
How is it that those who have the words

Are prone to praise the sour wind
Of violence? What of the innocents?
Perhaps the poet would tell me in sorrow
We all are culpable, that hurt makes
People wreak cruel yet beautiful havoc.
Listen, the romance of hate is singing.

GRADUATION

Waiting in a line and thinking back
To the mornings (countable but infinite)
By the roadside waiting for the bus
While the winter dark started to sliver

Into grays and silvers and how in winter there
Was snow-cushioned silence but on a morning
In May it would be light and there'd be bird song
Everywhere, a stop and start symphony,

And how the birds were up in the trees that just
Were starting to fledge with translucent greens
And how any one morning has its mindful weight
Because you are there, a little bird yourself,
As the smiling man gives you the paper and
You hear the cheers and then it's memory, again.

CONSPIRACY

Though TV makes public murders palpable,
Motives and planning remain arcane
To those suspecting minds that resent being
Left behind. "Nothing Is As It Seems" is

An old metaphysical tune and becomes
In quasi-reason's hands a sure virtue—
The CIA as cosmic Houdini. Longing
Eyes cast their vision on what can't be seen

And spew theories—the Mob, right-wingers,
Counter-agents, any lethal government.
Could be. Blame can pirouette seductively.
I've been mesmerized more than once.
My dad deliberates over pretzels and beer:
"Here's the truth, kiddo. Everyone's nuts."

MISANTHROPE

At first it was random moments—someone
Talking (snorting, really) about what someone
Had said about someone or an open mouth
While eating or a pile of flesh sedately mincing

Down the street. A nervous weariness accosted her,
As if forced to brook the same inane question
Again and again. When she took even
A brief look at the human news, it worsened:

Words and murders, words excusing murders,
Murders in the name of words. When she spoke,
She heard the whine and plaint in her own voice:
The illness of some tenuous ideal.
Whatever redemptive hope sustained her
Vanished. She wished hard for nothing.

60

MELANCHOLY

Weakness—the giving in to loneliness,
Refusing to let anyone else in, indulging
The blue perquisites of adolescence
Long past their sensible deliquescence.

He knew it but went on drinking and regretting,
Not calling up his friends and regretting,
Making scenes about nothing and regretting.
It all helped to make him sick of himself,

Which was, he knew, what he wanted. Then he was,
In his oblique way, free to saunter through
The city's brazen and quiet streets and imagine
The random lives and how the slim arc
Of feeling was pulverized. Back home, he put
On some jazz, touched himself, smoked, and rued.

HABERDASHER

Over the course of decades style changed:
Your regular Joe stopped wearing hats,
Polished brogues, ties, starched white shirts.
America became casual and drove away

From the store on the corner of First and Main.
Even Sunday faded. Over his after-hours Scotch
The retailer pleaded to his pleated wife:
"What can I do when gentlemen no longer

Are gentlemen? What can I say to a world of rubes?"
Each morning he tied a perfect Windsor knot.
Later, he stared disconsolately out the windows
At the busy cars, brightened when someone came in.
"How could you buy a suit from a stranger?"
He asked himself. Each advertised day replied.

SUICIDE

Couldn't resist, heard death stirring in
The next yard and looked around at the typical
Flatness of hot afternoon light broiling
The car, garbage cans, an ugly shade

Of green lawn chair. Couldn't resist the feel
Finally of placing his awkward breath in
His oddly calm hands—this, at last,
Is it. He shrugged with blank relief:

No more stuttered, sexual questions.
Couldn't resist the invitation of suddenness,
The plosive boom of emptiness, the spastic
Stop of it. People don't believe in sirens
Anymore, in voices that are bittersweet,
Dark, seductive, cruel, but he did.

RADIO

One educated voice—no drawl or chipped vowels
Or hurried elisions or wobbly ethnic inflections—
Is talking with another educated voice
About the Saudis. I think No Jews Allowed,

Camels, petro plutocrats, holy cities,
Kings, covered-up women. "Short-term strategy,"
One voice is intoning. I love how they calmly
Ratiocinate. Now and then, a bubble of wit

Trembles wisely. I could listen to their savvy
For hours—the semi-thinking person's narcotic.
When, for the hell of it, I push a random button,
The Mamas and the Papas are sublimely harmonizing.
They sound like angels on drugs. I sing too. Why talk,
When you can rise on longing's crazy wings?

ACKNOWLEDGMENTS

Grateful acknowledgment is made to the editors and publishers of the following journals in which poems or earlier versions of them first appeared: *Animus, The American Scholar, Beloit Poetry Journal, The Georgia Review, The Gettysburg Review, Green Mountains Review, Hoofbeat, The Journal, The Manhattan Review, Michigan Quarterly Review, Poetry East, Rattapallax, The Sewanee Review, Sou'wester,* and *Washington Square.*

Karen Dominguez-Brann

ABOUT THE AUTHOR

Baron Wormser is the author of five previous collections of poetry: *The White Words* (Houghton Mifflin, 1983), *Good Trembling* (Houghton Mifflin, 1985), *Atoms, Soul Music and Other Poems* (Paris Review Editions, 1989), *When* (Sarabande Books, 1997), and *Mulroney & Others* (Sarabande Books, 2000). He is the coauthor of *Teaching the Art of Poetry: The Moves* (Lawrence Erlbaum Associates, 2000), and works with students and teachers throughout the United States. He has received fellowships from the National Endowment for the Arts and the John Simon Guggenheim Memorial Foundation, and was appointed Poet Laureate of Maine in 2000. Wormser teaches in the Stonecoast MFA Program and at the Frost Place in Franconia, New Hampshire, where he codirects the Frost Place Conference on Poetry and Teaching and the Frost Place Seminar. He lives with his wife in Hallowell, Maine.